Leadership workbook for teens

HELLO
FUTURE LEADER!

I'm so glad you're here. The world needs more future leaders like you. We can't wait to see you do great things.

Use this workbook to set goals, capture your big ideas and hone your leadership skills.

You've got this.

you are one
in a melon!

HOW TO
USE THIS BOOK

This book is split into three sections:

Step one is all about setting goals and envisioning the kind of leader you want to be.

Step two is where you can hone the skills of a leader, build resilience, and a mindset that is fearless.

Step three is where you track your progress in becoming the leader you want to be

STEP ONE

Set Your Goals. Then Crush It.

LEADERSHIP Vision

My definition of vision:

Why is it important for a leader to have a vision?

My vision for being a leader:

Steps to achieve my vision:

LEADERSHIP *legacy*

My definition of leadership:

Qualities of a good leader:

-
-
-
-
-
-
-
-

A leader I admire and why:

My leadership legacy (how I want to be remembered):

LEADERSHIP *Qualities*

The top 5 qualities I believe are important for all leaders to have:

1 _____
2 _____
3 _____
4 _____
5 _____

Think of a leader you admire. What quality about them are you attracted to?

Leader: _____

Quality: _____

How they demonstrated it: _____

_____

_____

Think about a leader you don't admire, and identify the quality you don't like:

Leader: _____

Quality: _____

How they demonstrated it: _____

_____

_____

LEADERSHIP *Influence*

In its simplest form, leadership is **influence**.

Describe the relationship between leadership and influence:

Name and describe a leader who has used their influence in a *negative* way:

Name and describe a leader who has used their influence in a *positive* way:

Describe how you want to use your influence as a leader:

LEADERSHIP Teamwork

Define teamwork in your own words:

List three features that
make a great team:

1
2
3

List three dysfunctions
that break a team:

1
2
3

What quality do you think is most important for a team? Explain below:

Quality:

Explanation:

Write your favourite teamwork quote below:

LEADERSHIP *Relationships*

Explain why relationships are important in leadership:

List three essential ingredients for healthy relationships:

1
2
3

List three strategies to get to know people better:

1
2
3

Are the people you are leading growing as a result of your leadership?

Describe one change you will make to help you better connect with others:

What you do has far greater impact than what you say

STEPHEN COVEY

a strong

LEADER

is

SMART GOALS

A dream without a goal is just a wish. Have you heard this saying before ? Setting goals can help you stay focused on achieving the great things you set out to-do. Use the following worksheet to set your goals. Remember, no goal is too big!

SMART GOALS

Setting realistic and achievable outcomes.

My goal is:

S SPECIFIC | What do I want to happen? |

M MEASUREABLE | How will I know when I have achieved my goal? |

A ATTAINABLE | Is the goal realistic and how will I accomplish it? |

R RELEVANT | Why is my goal important to me? |

T TIMELY | What is my deadline for this goal? |

YOUR RESUME

You may not need a resume for a few years but now is a great time to start thinking about what you'd like your future career to look like. Use the following page to jot down some ideas.

MY FUTURE RESUME

NAME: _____   AGE: _____

LOCATION: _____

EDUCATION

⊙ _____

⊙ _____

⊙ _____

WORK EXPERIENCE

⊙

⊙

⊙

PERSONAL ACHIEVEMENTS

⊙ _____

⊙ _____

⊙ _____

CHARACTER STRENGTHS

⊙ _____   ⊙ _____

⊙ _____   ⊙ _____

Don't follow the crowd. Let the crowd follow you.

MARGARET THATCHER

IF I WAS
PRESIDENT
FOR THE DAY

To begin with, I will _____

_____

_____

_____

_____

_____

Next, I will _____

_____

_____

_____

_____

_____

Finally, I will _____

_____

_____

_____

_____

_____

Signed: Dated:

Your life is as good as your mindset.

UNKNOWN

HOPES & DREAMS

Fill your mind with your likes, interests, hopes and dreams.

STEP TWO

Crush your fears. Turn setbacks into opportunities..

The comeback is always stronger than the setback.

UNKNOWN

MY RESILIENCE PLAN

PEOPLE I CAN CALL OR TALK TO FOR HELP:

- _____
- _____
- _____

HOW I CAN LOOK AFTER MYSELF:

_____
_____
_____
_____
_____

MY STRENGTHS:

1 _____
_____
2 _____
_____
3 _____
_____

WHAT HAS HELPED ME IN THE PAST:

_____
_____
_____
_____
_____
_____

ADVICE I WOULD GIVE A FRIEND:

_____
_____
_____
_____
_____
_____
_____

When your values are clear, all decisions are easier.

UNKNOWN

YOUR BEST TRAITS

What are the traits of a good leader? Do you have them? If not, no worries! You can find opportunities and work on them. Great leaders continually strive to improve themselves. Use the following page to discover your strengths and traits to work on.

CHARACTER STRENGTHS

Character strengths are positive personality traits that help define the character of an individual. Have a chat with friends and teachers. Highlight your top 5 character strengths are and write about how you demonstrate one of them:

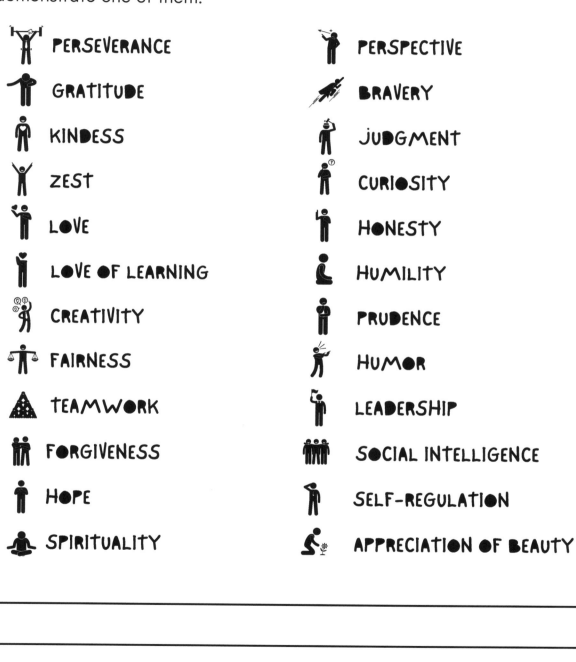

PERSEVERANCE

GRATITUDE

KINDESS

ZEST

LOVE

LOVE OF LEARNING

CREATIVITY

FAIRNESS

TEAMWORK

FORGIVENESS

HOPE

SPIRITUALITY

PERSPECTIVE

BRAVERY

JUDGMENT

CURIOSITY

HONESTY

HUMILITY

PRUDENCE

HUMOR

LEADERSHIP

SOCIAL INTELLIGENCE

SELF-REGULATION

APPRECIATION OF BEAUTY

_____

_____

_____

_____

Trust is earned when actions meet words.

UNKNOWN

Relationships TRUST

In your own words, what is trust?

_____

_____

_____

_____

List two things that can break trust:

1 _____   **2** _____

_____   _____

_____

What practical things can you do to build trust?

_____

_____

_____

_____

Is teamwork possible without trust? Explain your answer:

_____

_____

_____

_____

Who is someone you trust?

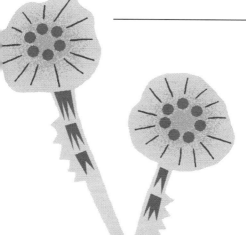

_____

_____

Your thoughts become your reality.

UNKNOWN

THOUGHT CLOUDS

In the clouds, write words to describe your thoughts when you have a setback.

You've got this.

UNKNOWN

Resilience STRATEGIES

Write strategies that you have used in the past, or could use in the future to help you successfully overcome a challenge.

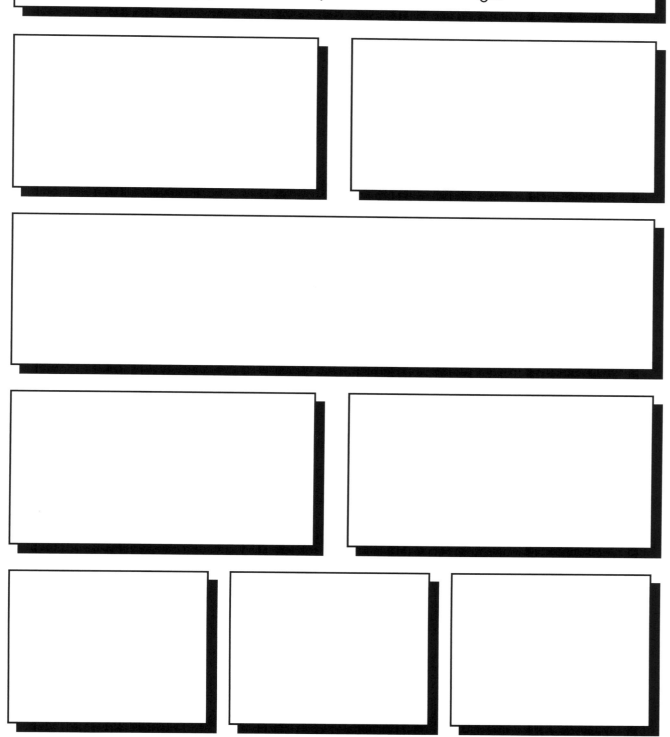

The one thing that overcomes hard luck is hard work.

HARRY GOLDEN

Mindset Language

Flip your thinking! Complete the speech bubbles:

Instead of: Say:

This is too hard!
I give up.

This is too hard!
I give up.

This is too hard!
I give up.

Every challenge is an opportunity.

Tricky Situations

Describe below your tricky situation:

_____

_____

_____

_____

_____

_____

_____

Replace yourself for a friend in the above scenario. What advice would you give a friend to help them out of the situation?

_____

_____

_____

_____

_____

_____

_____

REFLECTION

Every day you're presented with the opportunity to learn something new. Take the time to reflect after each day using the following prompts.

My Visual Journal

Read the prompts below and respond by filling each space provided with images and words that come into mind.

The best things that
happened today:

Things I wish I can
change about today:

I am proud of myself
today because...

I think I still need
to work on....

Create the soundtrack to your life.

MY ULTIMATE COPING PLAYLIST

We go through different positive and negative emotions everyday. It is okay to have all those feelings but we must also find ways to cope.

Fill each box with the title of songs (and their artist) that you think fit the descriptions provided.

FOR AMUSEMENT

a song that gets stuck in my head

a song I know all the words to

a song from my favorite movie or tv series

TO UPLIFT

a song I associate to freedom

a song that gives me energy

a song I'd like to wake me up

FOR DIVERSION

a song that makes me feel safe

a song that helps me think positively

a song that inspires me

TO DISCHARGE

a song for when you get anxious worried

a song for when you get angry or annoyed

a song for when you feel lonely or afraid

FOR STRONG EMOTIONS

a song that reminds you of a good memory

a song that makes you think of a loved one

a song to remind you that you are loved

SELF *love*

IN THE SPACES BELOW, LIST ALL THE WAYS YOU CAN SHOW
LOVE AND APPRECIATION TO YOURSELF

SELF *love*

IN THE SPACES BELOW, LIST ALL THE WAYS YOU CAN SHOW
LOVE AND APPRECIATION TO YOURSELF

Leaders are made, not born.

VINCE LOMBARDI

LEADERS IN ACTION

A PHOTO DIARY

Think about all the leaders you know. What do they look like? How do they lead? Draw and insert your photos here.

Write a few sentences explaining your choice of photo/drawings

We rise by lifting others.

ROBERT INGERSOLL

KINDNESS IS CONTAGIOUS

It feels so good when someone says something nice to you.. But often, we forget to tell someone when we think they have done a great job, or when we admire a quality in them. Choose four people in your class to write a kind, specific message to. Try to write one for someone who isn't in your immediate friendship group.

Principles of Non-Violence by Martin Luther King, Jr.

Martin Luther King Jr. was a Baptist minister and scholar. He was a social activist and led the civil rights movement against racial segregation during the 1960s.

Dr. King fought for equality and human rights for the Black people. He is also well known for his speech, "I Have a Dream," which he delivered during the March in Washington. In it, he said:

> "I have a dream that one day this nation will rise up and live out the true meaning of its creed: "We hold these truths to be self-evident, that all men are created equal."

He was highly influenced by Mahatma Gandhi's non-violent approach to protests. This lead King to write his six principles on non-violence.

In his book, Stride Towards Freedom, King listed down his six principles of non-violence as:

- A way of life for courageous people.
- Seeks to win friendship and understanding.
- Seeks to defeat injustice, not people.
- Holds that suffering can educate and transform.
- Chooses love instead of hate.
- Believes that the universe is on the side of justice.

Sources:
https://www.history.com/topics/black-history/martin-luther-king-jr
https://www.thoughtco.com/martin-luther-king-jr-1779880
https://www.youthinfront.org/nonviolence-and-protest.html
https://kinginstitute.stanford.edu/sites/mlk/files/lesson-activities/six_principles_of_nonviolence.pdf

Questions:

After reading the passage in the previous page, answer the questions below

Martin Luther King, Jr. was a civil-rights activist. What were the causes he was fighting for?

_____

_____

_____

_____

What are the benefits of using non-violent means for protests and assemblies?

_____

_____

_____

_____

Have you ever been in a situation that was difficult? How were able to resolve it?

_____

_____

_____

_____

Do not follow where the path may lead. Go instead where there is no path and create a trail.

HAROLD R. MCALINDON

DR. MAE C. JEMISON

Recall our class discussion about Dr. Mae C. Jemison and answer the following questions below.

What qualites does Dr. Jemison have that helped her reach her dreams?

Dr. Jemison said, "Don't let anyone rob you of your imagination, your creativity, or your curiosity." Why do you think these qualities are important?

Even now, a huge part of society sees gender and race as a hindrance to achieving goals. Why do you think that is the case? How can this thinking be overcome?

LEAD A PROJECT

Gather a team together to create your own masterpiece using the following instructions.

MY MASTERPIECE

A planning worksheet for your team project

WE ARE GOING TO CREATE A:

- [ ] Traditional Painting
- [ ] Digital Artwork
- [ ] Sculpture
- [ ] Collage
- [ ] Other: _____

WE'LL BE GETTING MY INSPIRATION FROM:

(an artist, a concept, a personal experience, another culture, etc.)

_____

_____

THE ELEMENTS AND PRINCIPLES THAT I'LL HIGHLIGHT ARE:

Encircle 4-5 items from the list:

line	form	color	space	variety
shape	value	texture	unity	rhythm
pattern	emphasis	balance	proportion	

HERE'S AN INITIAL SKETCH OF OUR MASTERPIECE:

The key to success is to start before you are ready.

MARIE FORLEO

You Can Be Anything!

Bessie Coleman wanted to be a pilot at a time when it was difficult for a woman and a Black person to do so. With her hard work and persistence, she overcame her challenges and reached her goal.

What do you want to be? Draw it in the space below.

What are the things you can do to help you reach your goal?

Write down the words that might block what you want to do... then cross them out!

ACHIEVE BIG GOALS

Big goals can be intimidating but if you can break a big goal into small steps, you'll be able to see and celebrate success along the way.

STEPLADDER GOALS

My goal is:

My end reward is:

Steps to success	Anxiety rating scale		Reward for success

STEP THREE

Think of a big goal you'd like to achieve. Now work towards it every day by taking daily action. See what you can achieve in just 30 days.

DAILY ACTION PLANNING SHEET

MAJOR GOAL

IDEA DUMP ZONE
(TO DEAL WITH LATER)

TODAY'S 3 MAJOR TASKS

1.

2.

3.

NOTES:

TODAY'S 3 MINOR TASKS

1.

2.

3.

NOTES:

DAILY ACTION PLANNING SHEET

MAJOR GOAL

TODAY'S 3 MAJOR TASKS

1.

2.

3.

NOTES:

TODAY'S 3 MINOR TASKS

1.

2.

3.

NOTES:

IDEA DUMP ZONE
(TO DEAL WITH LATER)

DAILY ACTION PLANNING SHEET

MAJOR GOAL

IDEA DUMP ZONE
(TO DEAL WITH LATER)

TODAY'S 3 MAJOR TASKS

1.

2.

3.

NOTES:

TODAY'S 3 MINOR TASKS

1.

2.

3.

NOTES:

DAILY ACTION PLANNING SHEET

MAJOR GOAL

TODAY'S 3 MAJOR TASKS

1.

2.

3.

NOTES:

TODAY'S 3 MINOR TASKS

1.

2.

3.

NOTES:

IDEA DUMP ZONE
(TO DEAL WITH LATER)

DAILY ACTION PLANNING SHEET

MAJOR GOAL

TODAY'S 3 MAJOR TASKS

1. _____
   _____

2. _____

3. _____

NOTES: _____

TODAY'S 3 MINOR TASKS

1. _____
   _____

2. _____

3. _____

NOTES: _____

IDEA DUMP ZONE
(TO DEAL WITH LATER)

DAILY ACTION PLANNING SHEET

MAJOR GOAL

TODAY'S 3 MAJOR TASKS

1. _____
_____

2. _____
_____

3. _____
_____

NOTES:

TODAY'S 3 MINOR TASKS

1. _____
_____

2. _____
_____

3. _____
_____

NOTES:

IDEA DUMP ZONE
(TO DEAL WITH LATER)

DAILY ACTION PLANNING SHEET

MAJOR GOAL

IDEA DUMP ZONE
(TO DEAL WITH LATER)

TODAY'S 3 MAJOR TASKS

1.

2.

3.

NOTES:

TODAY'S 3 MINOR TASKS

1.

2.

3.

NOTES:

DAILY ACTION PLANNING SHEET

MAJOR GOAL

TODAY'S 3 MAJOR TASKS

1.

2.

3.

NOTES:

TODAY'S 3 MINOR TASKS

1.

2.

3.

NOTES:

IDEA DUMP ZONE
(TO DEAL WITH LATER)

DAILY ACTION PLANNING SHEET

MAJOR GOAL

IDEA DUMP ZONE
(TO DEAL WITH LATER)

TODAY'S 3 MAJOR TASKS

1.

2.

3.

NOTES:

TODAY'S 3 MINOR TASKS

1.

2.

3.

NOTES:

DAILY ACTION PLANNING SHEET

MAJOR GOAL

IDEA DUMP ZONE
(TO DEAL WITH LATER)

TODAY'S 3 MAJOR TASKS

1.

2.

3.

NOTES:

TODAY'S 3 MINOR TASKS

1.

2.

3.

NOTES:

DAILY ACTION PLANNING SHEET

MAJOR GOAL

IDEA DUMP ZONE
(TO DEAL WITH LATER)

TODAY'S 3 MAJOR TASKS

1. _____

2. _____

3. _____

NOTES:

TODAY'S 3 MINOR TASKS

1. _____

2. _____

3. _____

NOTES:

DAILY ACTION PLANNING SHEET

MAJOR GOAL

TODAY'S 3 MAJOR TASKS

1.

2.

3.

NOTES:

TODAY'S 3 MINOR TASKS

1.

2.

3.

NOTES:

IDEA DUMP ZONE
(TO DEAL WITH LATER)

DAILY ACTION PLANNING SHEET

MAJOR GOAL

TODAY'S 3 MAJOR TASKS

1. _____
   _____

2. _____
   _____

3. _____

NOTES:

TODAY'S 3 MINOR TASKS

1. _____
   _____

2. _____
   _____

3. _____

NOTES:

IDEA DUMP ZONE
(TO DEAL WITH LATER)

DAILY ACTION PLANNING SHEET

MAJOR GOAL

TODAY'S 3 MAJOR TASKS

1. _____

2. _____

3. _____

NOTES:

TODAY'S 3 MINOR TASKS

1. _____

2. _____

3. _____

NOTES:

IDEA DUMP ZONE
(TO DEAL WITH LATER)

_____

_____

_____

_____

_____

_____

_____

_____

_____

_____

_____

_____

_____

_____

_____

_____

_____

_____

DAILY ACTION PLANNING SHEET

MAJOR GOAL

IDEA DUMP ZONE
(TO DEAL WITH LATER)

TODAY'S 3 MAJOR TASKS

1.

2.

3.

NOTES:

TODAY'S 3 MINOR TASKS

1.

2.

3.

NOTES:

DAILY ACTION PLANNING SHEET

MAJOR GOAL

TODAY'S 3 MAJOR TASKS

1.

2.

3.

NOTES:

TODAY'S 3 MINOR TASKS

1.

2.

3.

NOTES:

IDEA DUMP ZONE
(TO DEAL WITH LATER)

DAILY ACTION PLANNING SHEET

MAJOR GOAL

TODAY'S 3 MAJOR TASKS

1. _____

2. _____

3. _____

NOTES:

TODAY'S 3 MINOR TASKS

1. _____

2. _____

3. _____

NOTES:

IDEA DUMP ZONE
(TO DEAL WITH LATER)

DAILY ACTION PLANNING SHEET

MAJOR GOAL

TODAY'S 3 MAJOR TASKS

1. _____
_____

2. _____
_____

3. _____
_____

NOTES:

TODAY'S 3 MINOR TASKS

1. _____
_____

2. _____
_____

3. _____
_____

NOTES:

IDEA DUMP ZONE
(TO DEAL WITH LATER)

DAILY ACTION PLANNING SHEET

MAJOR GOAL

TODAY'S 3 MAJOR TASKS

1.

2.

3.

NOTES:

TODAY'S 3 MINOR TASKS

1.

2.

3.

NOTES:

IDEA DUMP ZONE
(TO DEAL WITH LATER)

DAILY ACTION PLANNING SHEET

MAJOR GOAL

TODAY'S 3 MAJOR TASKS

1.

2.

3.

NOTES:

TODAY'S 3 MINOR TASKS

1.

2.

3.

NOTES:

IDEA DUMP ZONE
(TO DEAL WITH LATER)

DAILY ACTION PLANNING SHEET

MAJOR GOAL

TODAY'S 3 MAJOR TASKS

1. _____

2. _____

3. _____

NOTES:

TODAY'S 3 MINOR TASKS

1. _____

2. _____

3. _____

NOTES:

IDEA DUMP ZONE
(TO DEAL WITH LATER)

DAILY ACTION PLANNING SHEET

MAJOR GOAL

TODAY'S 3 MAJOR TASKS

1. _____

2. _____

3. _____

NOTES:

TODAY'S 3 MINOR TASKS

1. _____

2. _____

3. _____

NOTES:

IDEA DUMP ZONE
(TO DEAL WITH LATER)

_____

_____

_____

_____

_____

_____

_____

_____

_____

_____

_____

_____

_____

_____

_____

DAILY ACTION PLANNING SHEET

MAJOR GOAL

TODAY'S 3 MAJOR TASKS

1. _____

2. _____

3. _____

NOTES:

TODAY'S 3 MINOR TASKS

1. _____

2. _____

3. _____

NOTES:

IDEA DUMP ZONE
(TO DEAL WITH LATER)

_____

_____

_____

_____

_____

_____

_____

_____

_____

_____

_____

_____

_____

_____

_____

_____

DAILY ACTION PLANNING SHEET

MAJOR GOAL

TODAY'S 3 MAJOR TASKS

1. _____

2. _____

3. _____

NOTES:

TODAY'S 3 MINOR TASKS

1. _____

2. _____

3. _____

NOTES:

IDEA DUMP ZONE
(TO DEAL WITH LATER)

_____
_____
_____
_____
_____
_____
_____
_____
_____
_____
_____
_____
_____
_____
_____
_____
_____
_____
_____
_____

DAILY ACTION PLANNING SHEET

MAJOR GOAL

IDEA DUMP ZONE
(TO DEAL WITH LATER)

TODAY'S 3 MAJOR TASKS

1.

2.

3.

NOTES:

TODAY'S 3 MINOR TASKS

1.

2.

3.

NOTES:

DAILY ACTION PLANNING SHEET

MAJOR GOAL

TODAY'S 3 MAJOR TASKS

1.

2.

3.

NOTES:

TODAY'S 3 MINOR TASKS

1.

2.

3.

NOTES:

IDEA DUMP ZONE
(TO DEAL WITH LATER)

DAILY ACTION PLANNING SHEET

MAJOR GOAL

TODAY'S 3 MAJOR TASKS

1.

2.

3.

NOTES:

TODAY'S 3 MINOR TASKS

1.

2.

3.

NOTES:

IDEA DUMP ZONE
(TO DEAL WITH LATER)

DAILY ACTION PLANNING SHEET

MAJOR GOAL

TODAY'S 3 MAJOR TASKS

1. _____

2. _____

3. _____

NOTES:

TODAY'S 3 MINOR TASKS

1. _____

2. _____

3. _____

NOTES:

IDEA DUMP ZONE
(TO DEAL WITH LATER)

DAILY ACTION PLANNING SHEET

MAJOR GOAL

IDEA DUMP ZONE
(TO DEAL WITH LATER)

TODAY'S 3 MAJOR TASKS

1.

2.

3.

NOTES:

TODAY'S 3 MINOR TASKS

1.

2.

3.

NOTES:

DAILY ACTION PLANNING SHEET

MAJOR GOAL

TODAY'S 3 MAJOR TASKS

1. _____

2. _____

3. _____

NOTES:

TODAY'S 3 MINOR TASKS

1. _____

2. _____

3. _____

NOTES:

IDEA DUMP ZONE
(TO DEAL WITH LATER)

_____

_____

_____

_____

_____

_____

_____

_____

_____

_____

_____

_____

_____

_____

_____

THOUGHT AND PATTERNS

Did you achieve your goal? What did you learn? Use the following pages to jot down your thoughts.

IDEAS

IDEAS

IDEAS

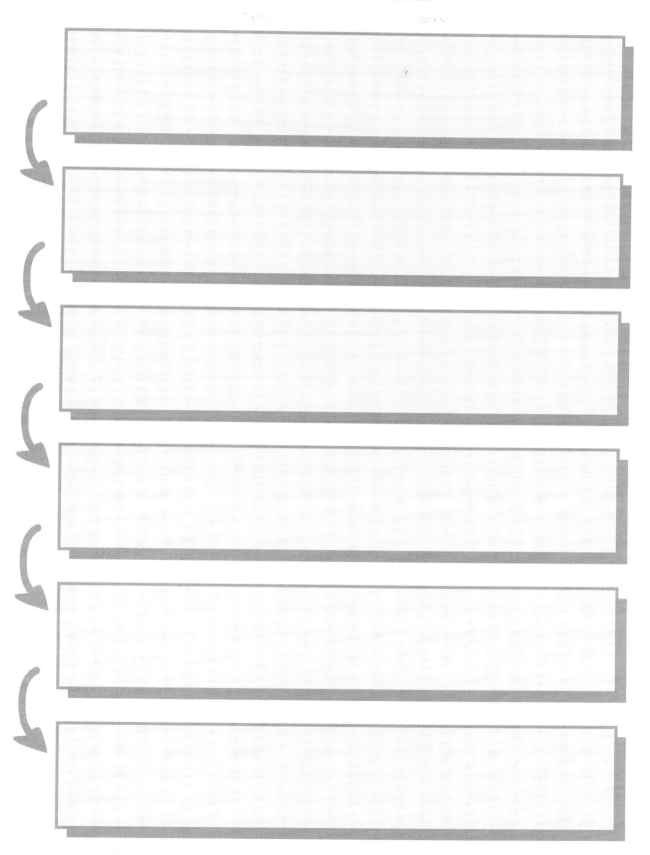

IDEAS

IDEAS

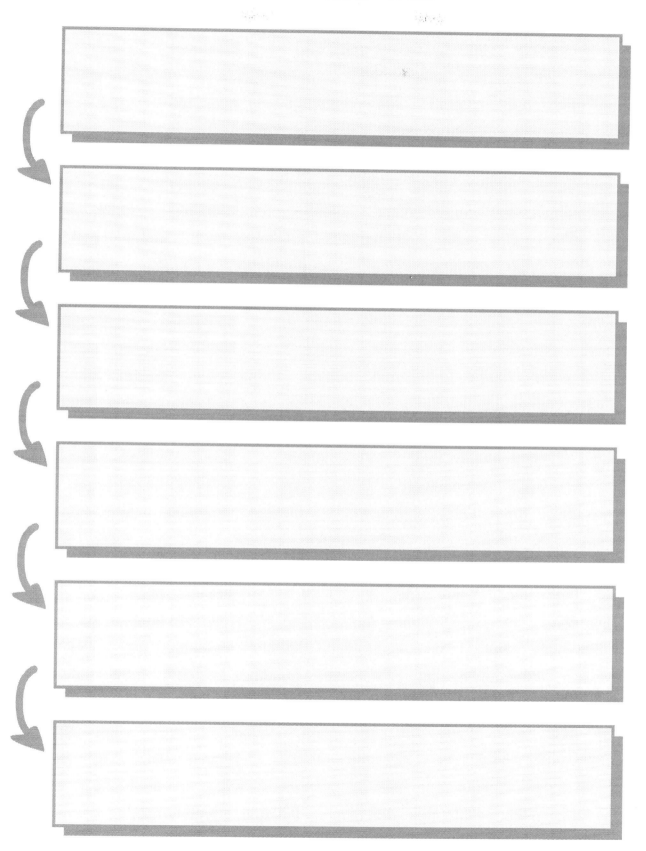

IDEAS